The Lor

an illustrated con
the Order for 1
Holy C

for
Common Worship

arranged by
Leslie J. Francis

illustrated by
Phillip Vernon

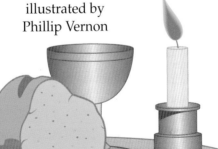

kevin
mayhew

The Gathering

In the name of the Father,
and of the Son,
and of the Holy Spirit.
Amen.

The Lord be with you
and also with you.

Almighty God,
to whom all hearts are open,
all desires known,
and from whom no secrets are hidden:
cleanse the thoughts of our hearts
by the inspiration of your Holy Spirit,
that we may perfectly love you,
and worthily magnify your holy name;
through Christ our Lord.
Amen.

God so loved the world
that he gave his only Son Jesus Christ
to save us from our sins,
to be our advocate in heaven,
and to bring us to eternal life.

Let us confess our sins in penitence and faith,
firmly resolved to keep God's commandments
and to live in love and peace with all.

Most merciful God,
Father of our Lord Jesus Christ,
we confess that we have sinned
in thought, word and deed.
We have not loved you with our whole heart.
We have not loved our neighbours
    as ourselves.
In your mercy
forgive what we have been,
help us to amend what we are,
and direct what we shall be;
that we may do justly,
love mercy,
and walk humbly with you, our God.
Amen.

8

Almighty God,
who forgives all who truly repent,
have mercy upon you,
pardon and deliver you from all your sins,
confirm and strengthen you in all goodness,
and keep you in life eternal;
through Jesus Christ our Lord.
Amen.

Glory to God in the highest,
and peace to his people on earth.

Lord God, heavenly King,
almighty God and Father,
we worship you, we give you thanks,
we praise you for your glory.

Lord Jesus Christ, only Son of the Father,
Lord God, Lamb of God,
you take away the sin of the world:
have mercy on us;
you are seated at the right hand of the Father:
receive our prayer.

For you alone are the Holy One,
you alone are the Lord,
you alone are the Most High, Jesus Christ,
with the Holy Spirit,
in the glory of God the Father.
Amen.

The Collect

The Liturgy of the Word

Old Testament Reading

This is the word of the Lord.
Thanks be to God.

New Testament Reading

This is the word of the Lord.
Thanks be to God.

Gospel Reading

Hear the Gospel of our Lord Jesus Christ.
Glory to you, O Lord.

This is the Gospel of the Lord.
Praise to you, O Christ.

16

We believe in one God,
the Father, the Almighty,
maker of heaven and earth,
of all that is,
seen and unseen.

17

We believe in one Lord, Jesus Christ,
the only Son of God,
eternally begotten of the Father,
God from God, Light from Light,
true God from true God,
begotten, not made,
of one Being with the Father;
through him all things were made.
For us and for our salvation
    he came down from heaven,
was incarnate from the Holy Spirit
    and the Virgin Mary
and was made man.
For our sake he was crucified
    under Pontius Pilate;
he suffered death and was buried.
On the third day he rose again
in accordance with the Scriptures;
he ascended into heaven
and is seated at the right hand
    of the Father.
He will come again in glory
    to judge the living and the dead,
and his kingdom will have no end.

We believe in the Holy Spirit,
the Lord, the giver of life,
who proceeds from the Father
and the Son,
who with the Father and the Son
is worshipped and glorified,
who has spoken through the prophets.

We believe in one holy catholic
and apostolic Church.
We acknowledge one baptism
for the forgiveness of sins.
We look for the resurrection of the dead,
and the life of the world to come.
Amen.

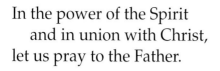

In the power of the Spirit
and in union with Christ,
let us pray to the Father.

Almighty God, our heavenly Father,
you promised through your
Son Jesus Christ
to hear us when we pray in faith.

Strengthen our bishop and all your Church
    in the service of Christ,
that those who confess your name
    may be united in your truth,
live together in your love,
    and reveal your glory in the world.

Lord, in your mercy
hear our prayer.

Bless and guide *Elizabeth our Queen*;
　　give wisdom to all in authority;
and direct this and every nation
　　in the ways of justice and of peace;
that we may honour one another,
　　and seek the common good.

Lord, in your mercy
hear our prayer.

Give grace to us, our families and friends,
    and to all our neighbours,
that we may serve Christ in one another,
    and love as he loves us.

Lord, in your mercy
hear our prayer.

Comfort and heal all those who suffer
   in body, mind, or spirit;
give them courage and hope in their troubles;
and bring them the joy of your salvation.

Lord, in your mercy
hear our prayer.

31

Hear us as we remember those
    who have died in the faith of Christ;
according to your promises,
grant us with them
    a share in your eternal kingdom.

Lord, in your mercy
hear our prayer.

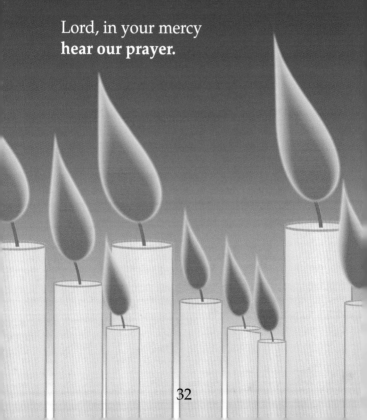

Rejoicing in the fellowship
   of all your saints,
we commend ourselves,
   and the whole creation
   to your unfailing love.

Merciful Father,
accept these prayers
for the sake of your Son,
our Saviour Jesus Christ.
Amen.

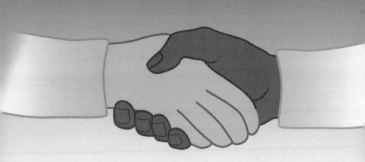

The Liturgy of the Sacrament

The peace of the Lord be always with you
and also with you.

36

Blessed are you, Lord God of all creation:
through your goodness we have this bread
    to set before you,
which earth has given
    and human hands have made.
It will become for us the bread of life.
Blessed be God for ever.

Blessed are you, Lord God of all creation:
through your goodness we have this wine
    to set before you,
fruit of the vine and work of human hands.
It will become for us the cup of salvation.
Blessed be God for ever.

The Lord is here.
His Spirit is with us.

Lift up your hearts.
We lift them to the Lord.

Let us give thanks to the Lord our God.
It is right to give thanks and praise.

Father, we give you thanks and praise
through your beloved Son Jesus Christ,
    your living Word,
through whom you have created all things;
who was sent by you in your great goodness
    to be our Saviour.

By the power of the Holy Spirit he took flesh;
as your Son, born of the blessed Virgin,
he lived on earth and went about among us;
he opened wide his arms for us on the cross;
he put an end to death by dying for us;
and revealed the resurrection
    by rising to new life;
so he fulfilled your will and won for you
    a holy people.

Therefore with angels and archangels,
and with all the company of heaven,
we proclaim your great and glorious name,
for ever praising you and saying:

Holy, holy, holy Lord,
God of power and might,
heaven and earth
   are full of your glory.
Hosanna in the highest.
Blessed is he who comes
   in the name of the Lord.
Hosanna in the highest.

Lord, you are holy indeed,
　　the source of all holiness;
grant that by the power of your Holy Spirit,
and according to your holy will,
these gifts of bread and wine
may be to us the body and blood
　　of our Lord Jesus Christ;

who, in the same night that he was betrayed,
took bread and gave you thanks;
he broke it and gave it to his disciples, saying:
Take, eat; this is my body
　　which is given for you;
do this in remembrance of me.

In the same way, after supper
he took the cup and gave you thanks;
he gave it to them, saying:
Drink this, all of you;
this is my blood of the new covenant,
which is shed for you and for many
　　for the forgiveness of sins.
Do this, as often as you drink it,
in remembrance of me.

Great is the mystery of faith:
Christ has died:
Christ is risen:
Christ will come again.

And so, Father, calling to mind his death
on the cross, his perfect sacrifice made
    once for the sins of the whole world;
rejoicing in his mighty resurrection
    and glorious ascension,
and looking for his coming in glory,
we celebrate this memorial of our redemption.
As we offer you this our sacrifice of praise
    and thanksgiving,
we bring before you this bread and this cup
and we thank you for counting us worthy
to stand in your presence and serve you.

Send the Holy Spirit on your people
and gather into one in your kingdom
all who share this one bread and one cup,
so that we, in the company of all the saints,
may praise and glorify you for ever,
through Jesus Christ our Lord;

by whom, and with whom, and in whom,
in the unity of the Holy Spirit,
all honour and glory be yours, almighty Father,
for ever and ever.
Amen.

As our Saviour taught us, so we pray

Our Father in heaven,
hallowed be your name,
your kingdom come,
your will be done,
on earth as in heaven.
Give us today our daily bread.
Forgive us our sins
as we forgive those who sin against us.
Lead us not into temptation
but deliver us from evil.
For the kingdom, the power,
and the glory are yours
now and for ever.
Amen.

We break this bread
to share in the body of Christ.
**Though we are many, we are one body,
because we all share in one bread.**

Draw near with faith.
Receive the body of our Lord Jesus Christ
which he gave for you,
and his blood which he shed for you.
Eat and drink
in remembrance that he died for you,
and feed on him in your hearts
by faith with thanksgiving.

Most merciful Lord,
your love compels us to come in.
Our hands were unclean,
our hearts were unprepared;
we were not fit
even to eat the crumbs from under
    your table.
But you, Lord, are the God of our
    salvation,
and share your bread with sinners.
So cleanse and feed us
with the precious body and blood
    of your Son,
that he may live in us and we in him;
and that we, with the whole company
    of Christ,
may sit and eat in your kingdom.
Amen.

The Body of Christ
   keep you in eternal life.
Amen.

The Blood of Christ
  keep you in eternal life.
Amen.

Almighty God,
we thank you for feeding us
with the body and blood
of your Son Jesus Christ.
Through him we offer you
our souls and bodies
to be a living sacrifice.
Send us out
in the power of your Spirit
to live and work
to your praise and glory.
Amen.

The Dismissal

The peace of God,
which passes all understanding,
keep your hearts and minds
in the knowledge and love of God,
and of his Son Jesus Christ our Lord;
and the blessing of God almighty,
the Father, the Son, and the Holy Spirit,
be among you and remain with you always.
Amen.

Go in peace to love and serve the Lord.
In the name of Christ. Amen.